Life Coaching

Guided

MEDITATIONS

By Petra Oblak

Transformational Experience

Content:

1. Authors foreword — 4
2. Love — 14
3. Morning Inspiration — 19
4. Evening Reflection — 24
5. Transformation and Accepting Changes — 29
6. Healing Your Body — 34
7. Healing Your Life — 39
8. Relationship Reflection — 45
9. Gratitude — 51
10. Values and Beliefs — 56
11. Overcoming Challenges — 61
12. My Goals — 66
13. Opportunities — 71
14. Fitness Motivation — 76
15. Dreams — 82
16. Giving — 86
17. Success — 92
18. Life Purpose — 95

About the Author

My Guided Meditations

are dedicated to all of you,

who took a moment in your life

to give and to love

Petra

1

Authors foreword

Aloha and welcome to the world of guided meditations, world of peace and tranquillity We all search for peacefulness and happiness. We travel the world in search for unknown. We look for gurus and Gods to answer our prayers and give us the answers. We search for the key to open the door, that is already unlocked. We look for answers, that has no question.

This book will present you with wonderful collection of guided meditations, that will help you to gather your own thoughts. Everything that we do in our life, begins with a thought. The foundation of our being and our life is a thought.

With the right positive thought we awaken our deeper understandings, and with deeper understandings the complete balance of our existence reappears.

Complete balance, Aloha Aina (brings a perspective to our life), is the purpose and meaning of this guided meditation book. Aloha Aina, is foundation for your true happiness, health and peace.

The underlining significance of this book is the Aloha Aina of our true existence withing our world and the universe, that was never separated and still is one reality of everything we feel, see and know. It is our own perception, created in our mind that has separated the reality of our existence. Meditations in this book are written in a harmony to help you balance your inner self, the world you live in, the life itself and the world within. Meditations are spiritually balanced with understanding of human needs, intellect and life coaching psychology.

Daily life as we know it, will only bring experiences to our life. Experience will bring knowledge. With knowledge will come understanding. Understanding will only be objective, if balanced with true reality of life itself.

Experience will bring the joy and the sadness, the pleasure and the pain. But the joy and sadness, pleasure and pain will always stay just an experience. The only change that can make a difference in our life and the way we feel about it, is the shift in our understanding, the shift in our awareness.

This is where the guided meditations will welcome you in to the world of serenity. Guided meditations will awaken the world that rests within you, the world that is your heart, your thought and you soul. It is the heaven within you, that lives with every breath you take.

Moment of quietness will build the rock solid foundation for your day, your challenges, your life and everything you intend to achieve in your life. Moment of quietness will increase your motivation, your strength and give you will power to live your life to your full potential.

I am frequently asked by my coaches and my readers and friends, what exactly is the mediation, what does it mean and how its done. So much has been written and said about meditation, yet for most people, this is still unknown and mystic experience.

Generally speaking, meditation is mental state, in which we attempted to relax our mind and enter deep state of awareness and inner peace. There are wide range of meditations available, or I should say, wide range of different techniques that will guide you into meditation state.

You should use the technique that is most suitable and one that you feel comfortable with. But all techniques have the same aim, to relax and connect with your inner self.

Some people will prefer a quite moment alone in complete silence and stillness. Some will prefer nice relaxing music, some require visual images to relax and some need guided mediations. For some reading and reflecting on the information given is meditation.

Being in a moment, being aware of the present moment is meditation. How to experience present moment and how to enter the state of meditation, that depends on you. Different people use different techniques.

Different religion will use different techniques to help on the path of faith. Buddhist meditations are widely used for spiritual growth. Christianity way of meditation is prayer. Islamic faiths way of mediation is prayer. The key to all faiths of this world is meditation.

To connect in a present moment, to connect with NOW, is meditation or contemplation.

Connecting with nature is mediation. For me surfing is meditation. For many hiking in beautiful mountings is mediation. Walking a on the beach, sailing. Writing and life coaching means meditation to me too.

If you are not sure what technique works for you, this guided mediation book will help you to discover your best way.

If you need inspiration to write your own guided mediations, meditations that will work for you, then this book will give you some ideas and will guide you.

Sometimes we just need a reminder of our life's purpose. Sometimes we just need to escape, sometimes we just need to BE. This book will help you to escape and help you to BE.

You can take short contemplation times whenever you feel like it, at any time of the day or night. You can be alone, or you can take moment even at work, on the tube, in the café shop. It is not so difficult to be alone and within, even if there are hundreds of people around. To tell you the truth, some of my best meditative moments I experienced when practising meditation in a noise place. You might find this unbelievable. Most people think you need peaceful and complete serene surroundings. I don't think so. Any place is good, busy and noise is fine, sometimes its even easier. With the noise going on around you, in your background, you can easier find your inner silence and peace. You should try it sometimes; you will see what I mean.

You don't need to have your home all to yourself to take time alone, you can find a space, and make it quite. You don't need to live your job and your life and move to the mountain monastery to meditate. You don't need to travel to India and dedicate 6 moths to meditation. Saying all this, you can if you wish, but you don't have to. It is your inner peace that will extend to the outside world, not other way around. It comes from within.

What I am trying to say is, you don't need anything or anyone to find a moment of peace and tranquillity. You are the place of peace, you are the moment.

Spend time with yourself, alone, wherever you are. At home, at work, travelling, walking, having a cup of tea, exercising.

My meditations reflect the spirit of Hawaiian Aloha, because it was on the North Shore of Oahu, where I found some most profound moments of serenity. It was Hawaii, that helped me to re-connect and re-discover. I wrote most of my guided meditations in Hawaii, in the presence of waves, sun, sandy beach and beautiful Hawaiian flowers. But I also wrote many meditations in London, during the coldest winter I can ever remember. It was snowing for most of the time during Christmas and well into the new year. In beginning of 2010, London was covered in snow, which brought the unique quietness to this busy multicultural city, that would normally spark from buzz. But the different ambience did not amend or change my inner peace. The cold London did not erase my Hawaii spirit of Aloha, as I have learned to accept the completeness of both, uniqueness and nonseparation of the worlds. I have merged them all within my heart.

So again, it all comes down to our own perception and our own inner world and how it reflects and connects with the existence, and with experiences of our life.

Remember that meditation and moments of peace, the time you take for yourself, is most precious time that you not only deserve, but need for your complete wellbeing, happiness, success, and awareness of your true meaning of life.

If you never took a moment of contemplation time, the following questions will help you on your journey of meditation. The journey that will mark the beginning of happier, more peaceful and more meaningful life.

I need "me time"
    I deserve "me time"
Every day there is a moment
    Waiting for me to unlock the power within.

Exercise:

1. Think of a person, it can be anyone from your life (parents, teachers, grand parents, spiritual leaders, children, your hero's).

2. Remember one of their pictures, or images, or moment you remember them by, where you could see them in complete serene happy moment. What were they doing? What do you think brought the peaceful expression, this great beautiful expression on their face? What made that moment memorable? Try to live the moment again, try to see the happy faces, happy moments. How do you feel?

3. Think of your own moments in your life. Moments, those give you the feeling of complete trust, unconditional love and balance. Think of a picture of you that you have that has captured a very happy face,

picture that expresses complete happiness and peace. What was that moment that brought the balanced happiness into your life? Try to feel it, try to see it, try to relive it yet again.

Moments like this, short, but powerful moments of peace we will remember for ever, these are the moments of meditative state. This is the moment the time stayed still, when the experience become unreal. It is that peace that makes the time stop, it is that moment that we capture. It is that moment that you entered into state of meditation.

If you have difficulties to relax or stay still, even with guided meditations and visualisation, then try to remember the moments of your life that shifted something in you or introduced new feelings to you at the time.
I would encourage you to look back at your life, and remember the moments; remember the moments where something magically appeared, something that stayed with you till today. Go back and remember people that made great impression on you, the moments, the pictures of others, your own personal events, the world events. Sometimes the sad events, people departing, people moving on. The time as we knew it, new beginnings. What were the moments that changed the way you think, feel or live?

I would encourage you to write down your experiences, as with remembering this experiences, you will connect again with your inner self, you will again awaken the feelings, you will yet again open the door to the truth of existence.

To grow, we must grow from our own roots. We can only grow from seeds we planed, from our own seeds. The grow can only continue from where it all began. Our flowers of love will only blossom when branches to cultivate them are ready.

So we must begin from our own roots, within our heart, in life that it is, the life that is us.

Boundaries of life, limitations of your abilities, restrictions of your world are braking as your inner strength is coming to light every time you take a moment to trust, moment to reflect.

                                                  Kindness & Aloha, Petra

It's TIME

for your contemplation moment
for the journey to begin
the journey to your inner self
the journey to your thoughts
the journey to your heart.

NOW is the time for YOU.

You are awakening the bliss that rests within
your deepest inner conscious,
The feeling of emptiness is slowly changing its
insignia,

without force.

With trust and we let go and release yourself
to the bliss
no force, just trust.
Bliss is appearing in every part of our
existence
ALOHA AINA

Come into view here and now
ALOHA IANA

2

Love

There is no evil in this world, it is just absence of love. There is no evil in our life, just absence of love. So there, we should not fight evil, we should focus on love, we should focus on bring the love into our life. We should focus on awakening love within our heart.

Whatever we attend in life, whatever we do, should be expressed through love. Love is not a word, love is the **action**, love is energy behind the life we live.

Whatever we set to achieve in our life, if intention is powered by the energy of love, the product, the result and effect will be love.

This is not as difficult as you might think. Empowering the love within, opening to the love that is us, is not that difficult and it can be achieved with meditation.

However, the challenge is in lack of love we receive, or the lack of love we want or need. We expect others to do loving things for us. We expect others to pass on energy the of love. This is not always the case, and the absence of love is a very painful experience, as we have all experienced it in our life.

We can choose to be loving, we can increase our love with meditation, we can systematically start introducing love into our actions and into our life. But we can not control the love that comes to us from outside, from other people. We can not change the way other people feel about us, we can not make others to love back.

This meditation will help you to awaken the love within, open up your heart and to heal the pain of absence of love.

We will at some point in our life, feel unloved, great pain will enter our heart, we feel the world collapsing around us. When this happens, we are in the mindset of greatest opportunity, our love within is stronger then never, our connection to diving is shining brighter then ever.

This meditation will help you to feel the pain, then will assist you to increase the love within you heart and extend this love around you, into your life, into your daily activities. With this meditation, no matter your circumstances, the painful experiences, the hurt and the pain, you will start recognising your ability to love, despite the pain.

> ***We can not do great things in life,***
> ***We can only do small things with great love.***
> ***- Mother Theresa***

In addition to meditation, we can start making small gestures of love. With small actions expressing love to others, we will start awakening love within our heart. To express love through our work will start awakening love within, love that we will feel, love that will comfort us. To express our love helping others, will awaken great love and increase our comfort.

We usually start looking for love when we loose love, when we are in unloving relationship, when we have no loving relationships, when we are lonely. Sometimes we have partner, we might be even married, but we still don't feel loved. We still feel lonely.

Spending time in meditation or reflection will open up your feelings. You will be able to feel what is missing, or you will be able to appreciate what you have. You will be able to feel what needs to change in your life.

It doesn't matter where in the cycle of love you are at the moment. You might be very distressed because of love loss, you might be unhappy, you just don't feel completely happy. This meditation will guide you towards the feeling of inner love.

It takes time to get over the loss of love. The pain we experience is the pain of absence of love. It is painful not to feel love in our heart. The common mistake we all make, is when we get hurt, we focus our intention on the other party, we focus on pain, we focus on absence of love. We re-live the events, good and bad, we live in turmoil.
Days of sadness and depression, are followed by long nights of loneliness. Tears and anguish. This is the moment, that we so often fail to recognise, how close we are to deep divine love.

The divine love is ready to shine and open up. But we are so involved in the despair, we lose the site of the true godly offerings that are available to us.

So to help you getting over the painful love experience, or the pain of isolation, we will travel to our inner holly place, awaken our true love. Our inner love will guide us and protect us. We will awaken the deepest love energies that we have never known before.

Meditation on Love:

I rest. I rest my body and I rest my thoughts. I am letting my thoughts flow through my mind. I let them be. I let myself be.

I am only focusing on love, the divine energy of love. I see the light of love emerging around me, surrounding me, entering my existence, my physical and my spiritual existence.

Divine love – the energy and power of pure, divine love – is building up around me and withing me. I can feel the shining energy of love warming up my heart, and I can feel the heat slowly covering by body, making me fee at peace.

I feel warm love in my body and in my mind. There is nothing else but love comforting me, holding me, hugging and caring for me.

With my loving thoughts, I create the love within. With my loving thoughts, I manifest the love withing. I feel the love, I enjoy every moment of this special feeling withing me, my life and in my relationships.

Love begins within. Love flows from my inner self. I accept my love, I share my love and I nurture my love.
I feel the birth of love, right here in my heart, right now.

Opening up my heart, allowing divine love to shine, letting the seeds of love grow and spread out of my daily life – this is the way I am welcoming the new life into my existence.

This is how I let love shine and grow from the depths of my inner self.

3

Morning Inspiration

Preparation for your day and your morning meditation:

The first moments, just after you wake up, will determent the way you will feel for the rest of the day. The first thought that enter your mind, when you wake up in the morning, will determent the course of the day. It is therefore essential, that, you take few moments of your time, and have a word with yourself. Yes, talk to yourself, first thing in the morning. Be gentle and kind to yourself.

The first words you hear in the morning should be the kind words of love. Welcome new day, say "Good Morning to me. Thank you my guardian angels for keeping me safe. I love you."

Stay with yourself, on your own as long as you can, but at least five minutes. If you can continue and take short meditation wile having your morning café or tea. The short moment alone will gather your energies, your thoughts and will reinforce your connection with divine, with your inner powers, your inner self. The bubble of energies will protect you for the rest of the day, the bubble of positive attitude will guide you through the day.

> "All that we are is the result of what we have thought.
> The mind is everything
> What we think we become
> -Buddha

Morning Meditation

I welcome new dawn.

I welcome new day.

I welcome new beginning.

I welcome new me.

Today I love, I live and I achieve.

With everyday break, comes new hope and new life.

With everyday break, the experience of yesterday, settles and changes into energy of knowledge and understanding.

Every experience of yesterday, good or bad, is no longer. The experience of yesterday has transformed into energy of understanding that can serve me well as knowledge for today.

There is nothing to hold me back, nothing to stop me. There is nothing to fear.

All there is right now, is new sunrise and new me, richer in knowledge and stronger in mind.

My confidence is at my highest level and I am now looking forward to today's events and moments that I will make today.

With the awakening of dawn, I shall carry on with me, through the day, the energies of power, strength and love.

With sunrise my motivation and confidence is set high. With every dawn my heart is filled with love, as the only experience of past, I fell is that of love. With every single sunrise, I captivate my feelings that serve me best and that bring me love and happiness.

I am now remembering all the blessings that life has given me so far.

I now remember all the blessings that I enjoy as a result of my hard work, commitments and the choices I have made. I give thanks for my strength and my faith now, as it is my strength and my faith that will carry me through the day with grace and with purpose.

I am letting go of all my worries and all my judgments. I am letting go of all my anger, all my sorrows. I am giving them to the rising sun. I see them rising up with sun, toward the sky, far away from me, far above, burning up in the heat of the sun.

My heart and my mind is overflowing with understanding, compassion and love. I have noting to fear as I take steps into the new day.

Today I am a new person and as a new person I shall take on new responsibilities. I shall continue with my daily duties passionately. I shall take the first step towards my new commitments; I shall take my first step towards my goals and towards my dreams.

I recognise my abilities and the great knowledge. I feel the strength and I feel the need to meet the challenges of my life. No challenge is too big for me. Whatever tasks I have been delaying until this moment, I will complete and deal with it today, with ease and with joy.

Starting now, I will keep my thoughts positive through the day, at all times. I will not think anything but thoughts of positive nature. No matter what the circumstances, the issues, the challenges, I will keep my mind positive.

My complete outlook of the world and life will be optimistic, and my day will develop and evolve in the best possible way.

Today will bring only positive outcomes in everything that I will attend, face up to, start or conclude.

My motivation comes from my positive state of mind.

My strength and power is within my positive thoughts.

When challenged, I will remember my affirmation for today:

I am upbeat, optimistic and no challenge is to big for me. I choose to see every challenge in a positive light.
I trust my life,
I trust my optimistic view.

4

Evening Reflection

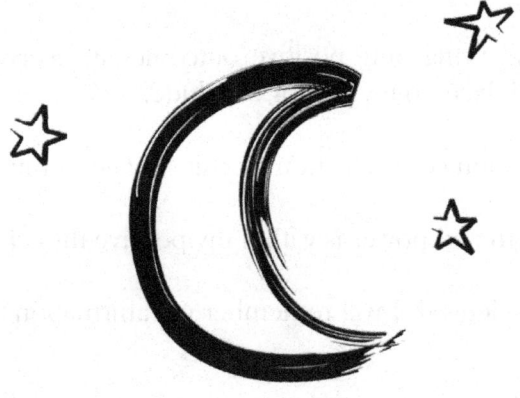

Preparation:

The day has come to and end, we are entering the special time of the day, the sunset, the peace of the evening.

Days are normally filled with busy schedules, work related stress, life's daily challenges. We might feel physically weak, mentally exhausted. Some days we might feel this way, the other day we might feel excited, happy and extremely pleased with the day's events.

Once you start taking time to relax for few moments in the evening, to reflect on your day, once you start taking note of your feelings, once you take stock of your day, you will be able to understand your life better, you will be able to really examen you life. You will be able to monitor your days, and see how many good days you have, and how many challenging days you have. You will be able to recognise the bio rhythm of your time and your life. By examining your life, it will be easier to introduce the right changes and to plan for future.

It would be great to wine down first, do whatever you feel doing, but it would be beneficial if you could take 5 to 15 minutes before you go to sleep to connect with your inner peace, gather your thoughts, clear your mind of all worries and prepare your body for a good night rest.

Evening Meditation:

As sunsets rests, in peaceful settings of the night, I too draw closer to a peaceful state and merge with peaceful energies of night.

My body, my mind, and my soul merge as one with power of the sunset, bringing together all my thoughts, all my daily moments, all my feelings. My heart can open up to cry or smile now, my heart can now speak to me and share its every emotion of the day.

Any stress or anxiety of today, can no longer serve its purpose now. I see all the stress and anxiety of today merging with the sun and closing with the sunset, disappearing from my view, melting with the sunset.

It is the time for closure. Closure to stress, anger, sorrow and hurt.

Nightfall is taking all, clearing my mind of negative worries and pessimistic thoughts. I shall not worry about anything right now, at the time of the sunset, I shall rest and balance with my inner self, my true existence so that the night can bring the dreams and love to my open heart and my clear mind.

I am now ready to embrace myself, my life and my experiences of the day.

The sun has set and day has passed, leaving me with the feeling of love, warmth and peace.

What good did my day bring to my life today?

All the events of today have now passed, leaving me only with the memory.

I am taking this moment of contemplation time to check my feelings. I let my feelings of the day surface. I let the feelings freely transform into the energy of love, peace and the sense of my wellbeing.

I am embracing all that was good today. I am embracing the progress and decisions I made. I embrace every moment that brought a smile on my face, every moment filled with happiness.

I embrace my relationships and love that is now established in my life.

My feelings flow freely with the energies of sunset. The transformation of the night, is generously purifying' everything, that no longer serves my purpose.

I deserve this time to reflect. I deserve this time of rest, time to rejuvenate and time to let go.

Night has come, bringing time of reflection.

Night has come, brining time for meditation.

Everything, that I no longer wish to carry with me tomorrow, I have freely pasted it on to the sunset.

Everything I love and cherish, I am keeping it with me, saved deeply in my heart. The night is blessing me with love and stillness of the nigh.

To be given an opportunity to reflect today, is a blessing and a gift. I am grateful for this time of grace. I recognise the immense strength and peace that comes from this evening meditation time. I feel the peace and love building up in my heart as the night progresses. I feel the energies of power resting in me, cultivating, and restoring.

I love. I am loved.

I love my body and I love the life I chose to live.

I love people I share my life with.

I love the night and I love the stars.

I love as I set myself to connect with the nigh.

I feel complete peace as the night sets to rest.

Night peacefulness surrounds me.

I lay in safe place that I can trust.

The blissfulness of night is now absolute.

The feeling of trust within me is expanding with the night, from within it extends around and beneath.

I am safe, relaxed, filled with love & trust.

The blessings of night,

in darkness I feel and see light.

It surrounds and protects,

shines down on me,

here and now, I feel safe.

5

Transformation and Accepting Changes

With every dawn your heart is filled with love, as the only experience of past you need is love. Every sunset is followed by the quite night, and every night is awakened by the sunrise.

The cycle of motion comes together within you, the motion of positive energy is the force within and around you.
The cycle of motion comes and goes. Cycle of motion brings and builds the feelings in your life. But only you decide what are the feelings and things you want to leave behind. What are the feelings that will set, together with the sunset, and never raise again when the daylight comes.

Only you decide what feelings stay, only you decide what continues in your life. Only you deice what are you wheeling to keep in the cycle of motion, only you decide what feelings will rise with you into your next dawn.

Accepting Change:

Change is the natural progression of life.

Change is undisputed and certain event of every form and very being.

Natural changes constantly occur in all earth elements.

Seasons bring changes in our world,

time brings changes in our bodies,

experiences bring changes to our understanding,

growth brings changes to our soul.

Every life form known to mankind changes over time. Some changes are permanent, some changes are temporary. Some are easier to accept than others, some take time to adjust to.

In our life, changes are inevitable. For some, changes are struggle, unwanted events that cases uncertainty and unfamiliarity. Some changes we generate ourselves, so we have some control over, but some changes just happen, they are out of our control. The only way to avoid the burden of those changes is to accept them.

As the changes are the natural progress of life, lets take them as the progression and opportunity that can lead to something new and something better.

The changes are like the endless cycles of motion, motions that constantly create and form new life. Sadness is never lasting, and joy will follow, tears of grief will stop, and tears of happiness will appear.

What changes will you welcome to your life today?

Cycle of motion brings and builds the feelings in your life. But only you decide which feelings you will hold on to, and which feelings you will let go off. What are the feelings that will set your motion to create new future.

What feelings will you carry with you today?

Cycle of motion brings and builds your character. But only you decide which qualities and values you will hold on to, and which you will let go off. What are the qualities and values that awakened in you? Which are the qualities and values that will set your motion to create new day for you?

What values will flourish in your life today?

Cycle of motion has increased your strength.

How will you direct this strength into your future?

We are all different. We all have different planes, we have different tasks, different priorities. We have different personalities and different needs. But in our true existence of life, we are all humans who face changes on daily bases.

Let us remember this as we move along our daily life, let us remember that deep down we are all searching for better life and better understanding. We are all searching for answers. We all have happy moments, and we all get sad and scared.

Our emotions guide our actions, but today, we will step into new life, with new understanding of life changes.

My commitment for today:

Today I will recognise and accept the changes that life has formed for me.

I will make changes in my life today that are necessary for my wellbeing. I will make changes that will improve my health, as health is necessary for my life.

I will make changes necessary to improve my character.

I will introduce changes that will bring happiness and love into my daily life.

I will push myself out of my comfort zone.

I will use my inner strength and power to make the positive changes in my life.

When challenged, I will remember my affirmation for today:

I fully accept the changes in my life.

Changes create better life, bring happiness, love and peace.

Changes are my direction signs to success.

I only accept changes which positively touch my life,

Changes which are good for me, my life and my wellbeing.

6

Healing your Body

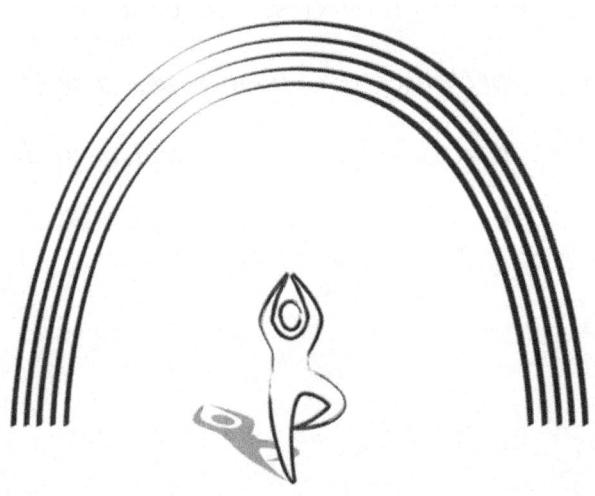

Rainbow healing meditation to heal your body;

With every breath I take, balance in my body is restored. My body is fully balanced, my body is in complete harmony.

Each breath I take, brings the Hawaiian Rainbow closer to me. I can see the rainbow closing in from the tips of my toes to the top of my head, manifesting the beautiful rainbow colours, covering the skies above and around me, slowly closing and coming closer.

With each continuing breath, I am breathing I the colours of the rainbow. With every breath the colours are entering my body, spreading slowly and gently, touching each inch of my body. The rainbow is now entering my lungs, my veins, my blood stream, making an entry into every organ and every cell of my body.

I can feel my body warming up. I can see the rainbow shining within me, within every corner and every part of my body.

I can feel my body warming up. I can see the rainbow shining within me, within every corner and every part of my body.

I am relaxed and I am enjoying the healing power of the rainbow. I am allowing the rainbow light to heal and to comfort my pain.

I feel the rainbow's comforting warmth and mist relaxing my body, making it stronger, healthier, and more balanced. The mist of the rainbow is filled with the sun's heavenly heat and cooled by the sprinkling rain of the moment, binding the sky and the earth into the power and strength that is me.
My complete body is powered by the strength of the rainbow. My aura is shining the beauty of health and strength.

Each colour of the rainbow is getting stronger and more powerful, touching and healing my body as it enters the new dimension of healing.

As the **red** colour of the healing rainbow empowers my body, its healing powers comfort my kidneys and my complete spinal column. As the red colour of the Hawaiian rainbow moves up the spinal column, the radiant healing light is making its miraculous flow, healing the body as it glows through me and around me.

As the **orange** colour of reproductive energy enters your body, the dynamic force of creation empowers my reproductive system, helping me flourish and creating a healthy balance, so well-being is now increasing within my orange beam of power.

The **yellow** colour of the Hawaiian rainbow is now shining stronger than ever. Its gold-yellow beam of light is shining, and its great divine powers are healing my complete nervous system. My nervous system is receiving the yellow light of calmness, peacefulness, and unique strength that is instantly releasing any stress or anxiety. I feel the golden mist spreading through me, and I enjoy the moments of stillness and relaxation. This moment will stay with me and will comfort my nervous system continually. As the golden yellow colour of the rainbow spreads within my body, its healing powers hold and heal the stomach, and it heals every tissue, every pain. The liver and bladder are surrounded, and the yellow healing power enters the organs with a gently healing touch. Yellow light is shining now through the pancreas, making its healing powers known and available to work with me, healing my body of pain and any discomfort that I may have experienced in my life.

As the **green** colour of the rainbow is making its manifestation through my heart, the blood caries the healing powers of green mist, healing the body with its every breath and its every heartbeat. With every heartbeat, the healing power of the green rainbow colours increases its strength and the longevity of the healthy body and its healthy soul.

The deep ocean **blue** light, shining the freshness of life with its pure, clean, healing power, is healing your lungs. You are breathing the light of life, the blue ray that is life, that is healthy, that is divine.

The blue Hawaiian rainbow light that I breathe brings the life, the love of life, and eternity to me now.
The thyroid gland is working fully, in great harmony, healed by the blue light of the rainbow, balanced completely now and in future.

Indigo is building up and attending its healing powers to my pituitary gland and every organ connected to its working powers. Balance, stability, and harmony are restored; indigo is now stronger than ever. The indigo power of healing is at its highest level. I accept the greatness and power of indigo, surrounding my head, opening up the dimensions, and taking my healing to the next level, the level of ultimate healing powers and healing strengths.

As the last colour of the rainbow sets upon my body, the **purple** spiritual, divine colour connects with my pineal gland, healing every organ and system connected and powered by the pineal gland.

All the colours of the Hawaiian rainbow are shining strong, transforming me into a healthy, strong, and loving being.

The mist, the light, and the divine powers are keeping strong, making the rainbow shine within and around me now.

I am still feeling the warmth. I am feeling increased vitality, and I am feeling the health and strength. I am keeping the feeling, holding on to that feeling, and I own it; it's mine.

The unity of the rainbow, with its celestial powers and its healing energies, is where I belong. It is where my home is. This is where I feel complete, and this is where my body heals, recharges, and gains its insights.

Blessed by the Hawaiian rainbow, I am shining in *Aloha Aina*.

Welcome to the tranquillity of my own world—a world that is me, that is power, that is timeless, and that is pure, now and always, in all different ways.

Relax and take a moment to contemplate,
                            take a moment to rest.

7

Healing Your Life

Rainbow Healing Meditation *Aloha Aina*- total balance

Relax. My life is a centre of energies created by my thoughts. I relax my thoughts, my thoughts are relaxed, my life follows in to relaxing state. *Aloha Aina* - I feel total balance of all my energies. *Aloha Aina-* I feel complete mental and physical balance.

As I relax, the light rain is continuing to draw closer across the sunny sky, as I relax even more, the shade of rainbow is slowly appearing across the sky. The halfway across the sky the rainbow's colours are coming more distinct, as I relax even more, the rainbow spreads across the sky, starching all the way from the ocean to the forest.

The Hawaiian rainbow is now if full few, overflowing with the divine healing powers. *Mana, Aloha Aina*

As I relax even further, the Hawaiian rainbow touches and connects with my *Mana*, my creative inner power, the greatest strength of my life. I feel complete spectrum of the rainbow connected with the energies of my balanced life. My existence and my life shines in the mist of rainbow healing colours. I see the misty colours surrounding my whole life. My life is now embraced by the rainbow, its healing powers and its eternal strength.

Let's now direct the attention to each healing power, individually coloured to enhance the distinctive part of my balanced life. There is a complete balance between the rainbow and my existence. There is only one energy that is created through the power of the rainbow, and that is the energy of love, balance, and healing.

As the healing powers of Hawaiian Rainbow stretches across the sky, touching my life with each healing colourful energy, stretched from red to orange, yellow to green, blue to indigo and rising up into purple, my life is touched by divine power that is now starting the process of healing.

The **red** colour of the healing rainbow touches the first *mana* centre, awakening my physical power and vitality witing me. The red colour of the rainbow is bringing me the security of the material world and stability. I am connected to Mother Earth, which is nurturing me and taking care of my basic needs. I allow myself and my life to open up to the healing power of the Hawaiian rainbow. As the rainbow touches the earth, my life connects with the earth and the rainbow via the first red healing colour of the rainbow. I am in balance with my life; The rainbow is taking care of my needs; the rainbow is looking after my well-balanced life. Life is good.

As the **orange** colour of energy and health enters my life, the dynamic force and emotions awaken my motivation and creativity. With motivation, I allow activities to take place, and my inner guidance is moving me forward.

I hold the power to my creations. My second Chakra centre is glowing in the pure orange healing powers of the rainbow, creating a healthy body, peaceful mind, and increasing my motivation, allowing me to rise above my dreams. I am healthy, my relationships are healthy, and I am secure and full of motivational energy.

Divine love brings the **yellow** colour of the rainbow to set in my third *mana* centre, lighting the love and kindness within me, bringing the compassion to my awareness, and increasing my personal power. I am optimistic and positive. My self-esteem is at its highest. I have a healthy view of the world, myself, and others. My life is balanced between my own self-nurturing and the kindness I express to others. Divine love shines within me, healing my life as a whole. My daily life is enhanced with personal strength.

The **green** colour of the rainbow is carrying the *Aloha Aina*—the complete balance and harmony—to my true existence. The green colour of the Hawaiian healing rainbow is strengthening my mind. I am receiving unconditional love that is endlessly flowing into my fourth *mana* centre, creating my inner peace and inner happiness, which is expanding and creating ultimate happiness in my life. My life is healing because the energies are continuously in my presence. My life is experiencing the power of unconditional love. I am in complete harmony within the green colour of the healing rainbow. The rainbow is touching my life with the remedy of its eternal powers.

Blue as the deep ocean, the blue strong colour of the Hawaiian rainbow is bringing the intelligence and logical thinking into my life, bringing the balance to my life and my dreams. The strong blue colour is speaking to me in a loving but logical way, reminding me of my mental power, my intelligence, and my strength shining through my life. My fifth *mana* centre is clear, and I express myself freely and clearly. I am aware of my thoughts and I think before speaking. My words are making the clear way for the actions.

The indigo colour of the rainbow is inspiring my deep wisdom. My spirituality and vision are coming to life as the indigo touches my forehead, healing my vision and awakening my intuition. I lay in complete harmony, listening to my intuition's guidance and its powers. I am connected to my inner self and the highest powers of creation; I trust my intuition, I follow it, and I act on it. You trust myself and I trust my life.

As the last colour of the rainbow sets upon me and my life, the **purple** spiritual, divine colour connects with mystical understanding. Giving me the powers of creation, this colour will lead me to my dreams and support my actions, and will lead me through my daily challenges. I am remembering my life purpose and the meaning of my existence. My life is in complete balance between my needs, my dreams, and my life purpose.

The colours of the rainbow are shining across the sky, lifting my life, and surrounding my life with the divine and healing powers. Whatever healing is required by my life, the Hawaiian rainbow has supplied me with the energies that are now, healing my life.

The light rain is continuing to move away from my life, light showers are slowly moving on, and the rainbow is slowly following the rain across the sky, glazed by the sun.

The colours are slowly fading away, one by one, slowly fading away from the sky. The sky is clear and sunny, but the rainbow colours are still surrounding my life and my daily existence.

Though the sky has cleared, and the rainbow moved on, within my life the rainbow colours are still shining, energising, and healing.

My life is constantly shining in the bright colours of the rainbow. The rainbow is creating a healthy and balanced life for me and my loved once, my life is filled with opportunities, love, and happiness.

Blessed by the Hawaiian rainbow, my life and I are shining in *Aloha Aina*.

Healing my life

Is healing my every moment

Moments make up my days.

I Focus on moments that matter,

moments that matter to me.

8

Relationship Reflection

*You can heal your relationship,
by healing yourself first.
Begin with yourself,
reflect,
and see your relationship heal, too.*

There is one more important fact to consider when we get into dealing with relationships, and definitely before we try to "fix them" or try to "fix or change" our partners.

This is why I call this part of the meditation book a "reflection" rather than anything else.

Every relationship has its ups and downs and its share of challenges. People change, and therefore relationships change, too. We are supposed to change, develop, evolve. But people don't evolve at the same pace or at the same time. Relationships don't always evolve the way we intend or plan.

As we live through the experiences of our life, we learn, we adapt, we grow. With the learning process we gain new expectations that sometimes are set too high, sometimes too low. We are forced or left alone to find our ways, moving along the life journey the best way that we know how.

Life is not easy, and life challenges can be cruel at times. If we have knowledge and support, we can deal with most difficult situations, and we can learn to deal with them. But sometimes we don't deal with the situation at hand; we move on, or at least we think we did, but some other challenge in later life triggers the unresolved issue, and we get even more confused and lost. If this happens in a relationship, we might be focusing on the wrong cause of the problem. We might be looking outside, or we might be looking at our partner, creating more drama, while the real issue is burning and hurting, dying to be healed, deep down in our heart.

If there is an issue in our relationship, let us reflect and let us find out why the current issue is so painful, why we are getting angry, why we are unhappy, why this relationship is not working, why all the drama?

Before making changes, before acting out, before hurting others, let us reflect. Let us find out who we really are, how we create our relationships, and why.

I stand on the pillar, made of my experiences,
Creating the pillar of love, so strong
That nothing can break it.

I stand on the pillar of knowledge,
Creating the pillar so strong
That nothing can change the course of my destiny.

I stand on the pillar of life,
Creating life
From what I know,
From what I feel,
From what I see,
From what I believe.

Relationship Reflection:

As sunset rests, in peaceful settings of the night, we too draw closer and merge with peaceful energies of night.

Our body, our mind, and our soul merges as one with power of the sunset, bringing together our thoughts and our hearts.

The sun has set, leaving us with our own inner voice, voice of our heart. The voice of the heart is speaking out, telling us our life journey, our memories, our sorrows, and our happy recollections.

There is aching past, left forgotten in our heart, trying to escape, crying to be heard, healed and understood.

Let us listen closely to the voice of our heart, and reflect on old painful experiences, experiences that hurt most. We are getting to remember those painful words, situations, experiences, people. There may be one, two or more of these situations. What are the old issues that are surfacing just now? What is your heart revealing to you now? *(write it down)*.

Issues buried deep into your past are adding to the pain of today. The only way to heal the pain of today is to heal the past, the feelings of the past, and the pain from the past. Let the issues surface, accept them, feel them, then let them go. Deal with them in your own way. Bring them to your attention, release them, and let them out.

What did the voice of your heart tell you today? What did it bring back into your life today?

Over and over again, the past is healing; the past is pain free.

All the memories that brought the pain back into our heart is healing. All the events of our life have now passed, they are now resolved, leaving us only with the vivid memory.

Let the vivid memory transform into the energy of love and peace.

Let the love create our life today. Let the love be focus of our life. Let the love be the creator of our relationship, as only love can create and last. Relationships created by love can never be destroyed, as love is strong, and love is endless.

Do you feel love within your heart?

Do you feel love in your relationship?

Is love creating the power that is needed to maintain the relationship, the long-lasting commitment, respect, trust, forgiveness, acceptance, and honesty?

Make your love so strong that love itself will show you the way and shine on the road that you are intended to take—the road towards complete happiness, the road of life that is love and is you.

Only with the love that comes from love will your love grow into eternity. Only love that gives will take you on its wings and show you the life in the eyes of ultimate acceptance and happiness.

Free up your feelings with the energies of sunset, and the transformation will generously purify everything that no longer serves your purpose. You deserve the time of rest, time to rejuvenate, time to reflect, and time to love—love with your heart and your soul.

9

Gratitude

Gratitude is one of the simplest ways to create a power so strong within yourself, that it will build whatever you desire in any area of your life.

Gratitude is the most powerful tool that will assist you in reaching for your goals and will bring strength into your life.

Gratitude is a ladder to your dreams—so easy to set in place, so easy to climb.

Its so easy to say "thank you" for everything that you have. It is also important to say "thank you" for everything that you have lost, and everything that is yet to come. Say it. Say "thank you" to the Creator of life. Say "thank you" to everyone that makes the days of your life comfortable, safe, and filled with opportunities.

How do you feel? How does it feel to be grateful? Yes, it feels great. Furthermore, the gratitude state of mind is positive mind, happy mind, creative mind.

More difficult to say it, but therefore that much more powerful, is the gratitude for things in life we don't appreciate, we don't want, such as pain, problems, illnesses, difficulties, losses and other hardships in our life.

Can you rise above and say "thank you" to everything, absolutely everything in your life? Can you grow over this barrier and see everything in your life as a part of life that simply is?

Are you ready to take this huge step and say thank you to things that caused you hurt?

Remarkably you will feel the relief, you will be able to let go of anger or hurt and you will be able to raise above and move forward, all because of a simple "Thank you".

It's a miraculous word, miraculous statement.

Thank you.

Gratitude Meditation:

Despite of our current circumstances in our life, in spite of perhaps a slight imbalance or possible upsetting feelings, despite of the likely struggles of our daily life, we are now taking a short contemplation time for gratitude.

Though there are situations, people, and issues that need attention in our life or perhaps require changes and adjustments, we shall not focus on things we need to change or improve right now.

We are now letting go of all our worries. We are turning away from the challenges, problems, pain, and stress. We are turning our back on situations that create tension in our bodies, ache in our hearts, and despair in our lives.

Let us *not* grieve for the things which we do not have, but let us celebrate things that we do have. Let us not cry for the things we have lost, but let us be glad for what we have found.

Right now, right this moment, we are turning our focus on gratitude and the appreciation of our existence. We accept our body, our life, and our being as they are—as they are right now.

We accept our individuality; we recognize it as a perfect form in a perfect state.

We are thankful for the opportunity to have peaceful time to reflect on our inner self. We are grateful for the choices we have made in past, because they lead us into this current moment or state.

We are thankful for opportunities we have been given and for free will. It is free will that brings our dreams into existence. It is free will that allows us to choose the right path, and it is the right path that takes us to our chosen life. We are thankful for this freedom of choice and freedom of life.

We are grateful for our past, we are grateful for today, and we are grateful for the life that tomorrow will bring. We shall accept the coming life with gratitude.

We are thankful for every challenge, every pain, every shed tear, and every sorrow, as they have contributed to our strength and our character and awakened compassionate feelings in our hearts.

We are thankful for every moment that brought us happiness and every moment that brought us sadness.

We are grateful for all the pain caused, intentionally or unintentionally.

We are thankful for every person that loved us, and every person that hurt our feelings and brought pain to our heart. Let each person be blessed by the love of the Creator. We are thankful for all the feelings that set our life in different motions. We accept that feelings are the motion of energy that changes and travels in waves of changing tide.

We are thankful for health and love that inhabit us every moment of our life.

As our day progresses, we shall remember to say the magic words with every challenge and with every happy moment of the day. We shall remember to say:

"Thank you; my life is just the way it is meant to be. Thank you." My life experiences are what made me who I am today. I am a strong and grateful human being. Thank you for my life, though imperfect at times, it is exactly as it should be. Life brings me challenges, challenges bring me strength which make my dreams come true.

Thank you for everything and everyone.

I woke up this morning

thanking creator for everything that I have,

and for everything that I don't have.

I am going to bed tonight

Thanking creator for everything

that is still to come.

10

Values and Beliefs

Our Values and Beliefs Meditation

Stunning flowers of Hawaiian bloom in this tropical sunny island of Oahu in the midst of the Pacific Ocean. Peace and bliss are all we feel. Fed with rain pure and gentle, flowers blossom in the breeze.

Imagine every flower that you see symbolizes one of your true values—the values that blossom in the depths of your heart.

Let these values blossom, and let them shine in the light of the sun. Let them fly in the wind and let them brighten up your life.

Enjoy the beauty of your values; see them gracefully brightening your life, attracting butterflies that bring they joy and colour to your life.

What do you see? Red flowers of love and friendship, white flowers of truth and peace. What values are flowering for you now?

Let them flourish. Feel that value you call love, feel that value you call the truth, feel that value you call family. Accept your ethics and your moral values, and thank them for existing, as they create your life of virtue and worth.

Are there any blossoms of values still waiting to flower and to craft your life into a garden of paradise? Send your loving thoughts to them and they will awaken and blossom, and, with them, your life, your health, and you will blossom, too.

See the tree living and growing for hundreds and hundreds of years, feeding the leaves high above the ground through its branches and its roots.

What beliefs does this tree hold, standing there throughout its existence, growing through storms and nature's evolution, encouraged by the sun shining through rainbows, and blessed by the moon?

What beliefs have kept it going through all its living days?

I am strong and I am tall.
I know that all I need is provided by God's grace.
I need not fear.
I accept and give freely.
I love and I receive love freely.

What are your beliefs that grow within your deep roots?
What beliefs has your life generated for you?
Every change and every growth—what beliefs did they generate for you?
Let them flow.

Any weeds of negative beliefs, let them show, let them surface. Touch them, feel them, then pull them up and throw them away to allow your values grow.

Plant the encouraging and positive beliefs that will help you grow and let you shine in the glory of your life, your work, your health, your wealth.

I hear you...I hear...
I am loved.
I am accepted.
I am.

My health and strength are greater than the ocean. My beauty shines in the divine light of today.

I grow high into the sky.

I am sitting on the rainbow of my values and beliefs that protect me on my journey from earth to heaven, from heaven to earth, and on my life's journey.

I am safe.

I believe I can do it.

I believe I can make it.

I believe so,

because I know so.

Because I have done it before.

I know the power is within me. I decide what I do, when I do it, and how I do it. I know the way to my happiness. My thoughts are always positive and empowering. Positive thoughts create my ideas; my ideas create my reality.

When I am calm, I make the right choices. When I trust the process of life, life trusts me with love. Harmony surrounds my existence within, and around me there is the light of protection.

I express gratitude for all that I am, all that I have, and all that I do.

I make choices that are good for my health, good for my mind, and good for my soul.

I blossom in the wideness of my talents.

I am safe and secure.

I am making positive changes.

My life has meaning and purpose.

I always make the right choices.

I am guided by my values, and my thoughts are positive and pure.

I build my life on solid ground, which I call my values.

I am strong and tall.
I know that all I need is provided by God's grace.
I need not fear. I accept and give freely.
I love and I receive love freely.

11

Overcoming Challenges

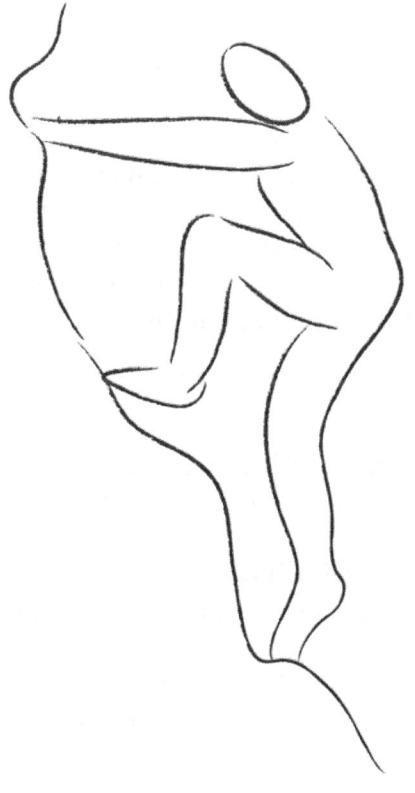

As the sun prepares to set, the peace and harmony is gently embracing around us. The orange rays of serene energies are softly reflecting in our mind, our body and in our soul.

Each time the sunset divine light dissolve away all our worries and blesses our souls with peaceful rest.

It is time now to rest all our worries, our challenges, our problems, all the issues and all that is not of our higher self, all that we recognise as an obstacle, things that we know no longer serve our purpose.

Think of all the challenges that life created for you today.

Bring them to your awareness, feel them..... what are they? What are all the issues that made you sad today, that made you give up your purpose today? What brought you stress and anxiety today? Who made obstacles for you today?

Let all the problems surface, say them laud...... as you think of the challenges, as you think of your issues, as you say them or feel them, they are lifted by the orange beam of light, see them flowing and then gradually fading away with the sunset. Dissolving in a hit of the sun, vanishing ... disappearing..........

You are calm and with one deep breath all the tension is lifted.

Surrender every thought and every feeling that is not of your pure love to the sunset......now.

Life is a long line of events and changes. And every change and every event will bring along its challenges. There is no escape, and you don't want to escape.

All you need to do now is to relax at this blissful time of divine sunset energies, and think:

What can I do differently tomorrow?

What can I do to avoid getting the same situation, same problems tomorrow?

What can I do differently tomorrow?

What will I do differently tomorrow?

What else can I do differently tomorrow?

As the sunset is blessing your inner strength and increases your divine powers, the positive thoughts are coming to your mind.

    Let them be.   Let them be.

What addictions and bad habits am I holding on to?

Am I prepared to release them now?

We can't hide from our higher self.

The only person you can fully trust and the only person you need to be honest with, is yourself. Look deep into your heart now while the sunset ray of light is healing you, and uplift all your addictions, all your bad habits, everything that you feel is bringing about challenges, situation, obstacles and feeling of unhappiness and loneliness.

Feel them …bring them to your awareness, feel them….. what are they. What are all the addictions and bed habits that made you sad today, that made you give up your purpose today?

Let them out, say them laud...... as you think of the them, as you think of your addictions and specific behaviours, as you acknowledge them - they are lifted by the orange beam of light. Now see them flowing and gradually fading in the sunset. Dissolving in a hit of the sun, vanishing ... disappearing.... ......

Relax and bath in this blissful time of divine sunset energies and think:

What can I do differently tomorrow?

What can I do to avoid getting hurt?

What will I do differently to avoid getting hurt?

What can I do tomorrow to take a step in a different direction?

As the sunset is blessing your inner strength and increases your divine powers, the empowering thoughts are coming to your mind.

Let them be.   Let them be.
Trust your inner voice.

Take notes of your thoughts and keep them with you until the area of your concern is resolved, until the challenges are met and situation is healed. Keep the card with you as a reminder. Every time you will hold the card, the power of sunset will be with you to help you on your journey.

Feel love. Feel sunset embracing you and holding you in comfort and safety.

*You are loved - always, in all your situation,
with all your habits,
with all your addictions,
all your issues.*

You are loved – always.

12

My Goals

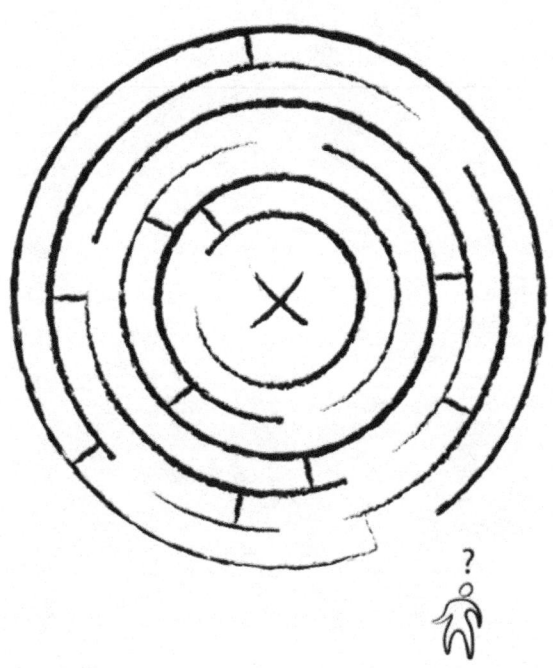

Welcome on our journey, our voyage of discovery, discovery of our goals. We are flying over the landscape and ocean shores of North Shore of Oahu. Our journey is taking us along the shore. Where are we flying to? Do we now? Our route is planed.

We need to know how long the journey will last, to insure we have enough gas. We need to know direction of our trip. Tropical Island is small, we can cross in within 20 minutes. With the view of the sky and beauty of the ocean, we could easily loose track of time, track of purpose, track of our destination.

We could just let go and enjoy, let our feelings merge with peaceful scenery, keep flying and flying without any worries. Nothing would stop us, no barriers, not challenges. Sky is clear, no winds not a cloud. And before we could even realise it, we could be in the middle of Pacific Ocean, only waking up from our day dream, when our flying bird has lost its power.

What would do we do then?

Our journey of life can be just like this. We can so easily forget what once was our dream, what once was our goal, what once were our values. We let got and we fly, we get couth and forget where we were going.

We might have our end destination in our mind today, but we get occupied by our life's issues and other situations, other priorities of the day take over our life.

We mustn't let this happen. We must still enjoy the journey but we must know where we are going. We can stop somewhere, and have some fun, as long as we get back on track afterwards. By planning our journey and by setting our end goals, following our plan, we can enjoy the life journey even more.

Just imagine, the road map, marked with stops, resting places, short stops, longer stops, small goals, big goals. So much easer to manage.

How different the shore looks from far above. If I needed to plan the journey, it would be so much easer to plan it from here. I can see so much clearer. I can see starting point and I can see my end point of my journey. I can see spirals; I can see hills, the trees, the traffic. I can see the road I ride and drive every day. How different it looks from far above, how different it looks from different perspective, yet it is the same road.

There are so many different views we can take in our life, different views of our goals, our journey. If we can't see clearly from where we are, why not step away, imagine yourself flying high above, take different perspective of your life. See things different, see it throw different eyes. Sometimes this is all you need to see your life journey with clear view, sometimes just taking different stand will solve your issue.

With your destination in your mind, what does your journey looks like. Of course you might have to cross bridges, clime the mountains, swim across lakes and travel through storms. But, can you see yourself enjoying the journey? Can you see shortcuts? Can you see highways? What do you see on your life journey, what final destination can you see?

Will you have to compromise and give up something of your core value, give up something you love to get to your final destination? Is this really what you want?

Is there something you can't take with you on this journey?

Our flying bird is small, I couldn't take my family with me to see this paradise, thought I really wanted it to. But I know I am coming back and can make another journey. Can you? Can you go back once you reach your destination, and find your world steel unchanged, waiting for you.

Whatever your journey of life is, make it safe and make it enjoyable. Get prepared to know your road, get started with your end destination in your mind.

Let your heart be your guide,

let your mind be your guard,

let your soul be your overseer.

Take your breaks, take your stops, take your time to look back, take your time to check your course. Do whatever it takes to insure you are moving towards your goal. Ask for help, ask for directions, but never ever give up. There is no U turn on the journey of life. Let your energy flow freely, re-direct them but don't try to stop them.

Don't force them the wrong way.

Follow your heart and use your mental power for guidance.

You will know when you are on the right part.
You will know!
Trust your inner self.

PS: Big hug and thank you, to my dear good friend Alan Sitt, of Sunset Beach, Oahu, for a safe ride in that "bird" on that sunny afternoon... its good to feel safe, and I did feel safe flying with you.
Aloha

13

Opportunities

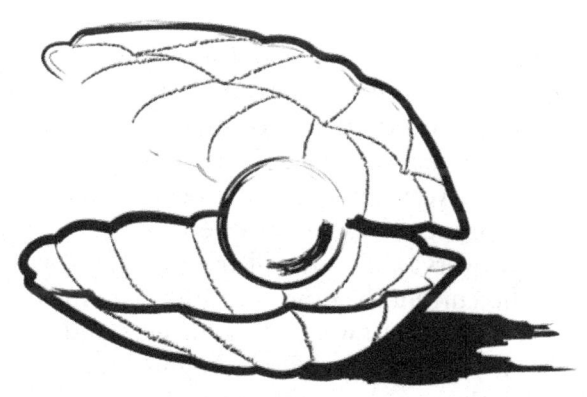

"An unexamined life is not worth living."

Socrates

The ocean is vast and immense; we can't even see the end. How massive is the ocean, and how much power and energy are stored in this vast amount of water?

Imagine the harmony that is required for the ocean to move, for the tide to change, for the current to shift in total **perfection.**

How much harmony is necessary for the waves to appear in their perfect form—the different sizes and with immense but perfect power? Imagine the energy that holds all this mass in order—energy that moves and stirs from the great depths to the gentle surface of it all.

If your opportunities were hidden on the ocean floor, in the ocean waves, and in the ocean depths, would you be able to account for them, for all of them? Could you find and account for all of them?

The opportunities in your life hold the same greatness and same immenseness as the ocean. No more, no less. Your opportunities are everywhere—so many you could never count them all, they are endless. You might not see them at the first glance, as you cannot see the ocean's depth, but you know they are there. You might have to dive, to go on the journey of discovery, and you will have to wait for the right tide and for the current to come your way. You might have to wait, but you will have to wait with your eyes and your mind opened to see them, so you can recognise them and seize them when life delivers them onto your shore.

There is only one energy that joins the opportunities for a better life, and it's the energy of love. Opportunities are like pearls collected on the string of love. Sometimes the string stretches, and it takes longer for one's opportunities to come by, but as we reach for one, another appears, and then another, and all we need to do is accept them with gratitude and love.

After the storm the ocean waves carry all these beautiful shells onto our shores. We pick some. Different people collect different shells. Some people I know collect sunset shell, and some pick puka shells to make jewellery. I collect corals in the shape of a heart. We collect what we relate to, what we reflect, what we need, what we want. I never knew there was sea glass down our shore. I thought you need to go some special place. Then my good friend Roger told me, "There is plenty of sea glass everywhere; you just need to look for it." And the next time I walked the beach, I did look for sea glass, and I found one piece, then the second, then the third, and so on. I found many pieces. I saw them because I knew they were there.

You need to look to see. You must believe its there, to see it.

What if the shells were our opportunities? Which ones would you collect? Would you wander down the beach, find what you like or need, but then not collect it? Would you look at it, lying there in the sand, and not be bothered to pick it up? Would you be too selective, and none of them was right for you? Would you wait for more to come next day, and again next week, next year? Would you stop looking, stop believing they are there?

Sometimes we are like this, too. Then time passes and we are wondering; what would have happened if I had picked up that shell? What would happen if I have chosen that opportunity in my life? How would my life be different? Have I made a mistake when life presented opportunities to me?

Don't be one of those people who wonder: What would have happened if I made a different choice? Why did I let my life's opportunities pass me by? I misted out.

You will never know when the next big storm will stir the ocean and bring new opportunities your way. You never know when the current will change, so take opportunities when they come your way.

The energy of love expands. The more you interact, the more energy of love will come your way, bringing an endless string of opportunities.

Be ready. Be awake. Listen to your heart; is the ocean of love flowing thought your heart, surfacing the endless supply of shells?

Take them, one by one, line them up, arrange them, make them create your life, and let them bring love, happiness, satisfaction, and beauty to every moment of your life.

But if you missed some, don't despair. We all do. We all wandered around looking and looking, but not seeing at all.

Wait; the ocean is rich, and there is no end to opportunities—there is no end. There will always be an immeasurable quantity of opportunities, and you will take the ones that are right for you, when the time is right.

Let the ocean rest and let yourself enjoy the stillness of this life. The preparation time is necessary. Rest time is essential, and the energy flow of opportunities comes and goes as our life's purpose requires it too.

The ordering process of your dreams and delivery process of your dreams are in harmony, the same as the ocean's movement and the movement of life.

I believe in opportunities,
    I believe my life is presenting the opportunities
        to me every day.
I am brave and I take the opportunities,
    They change my life for better.
        I am always moving forward

14

Fitness Motivation

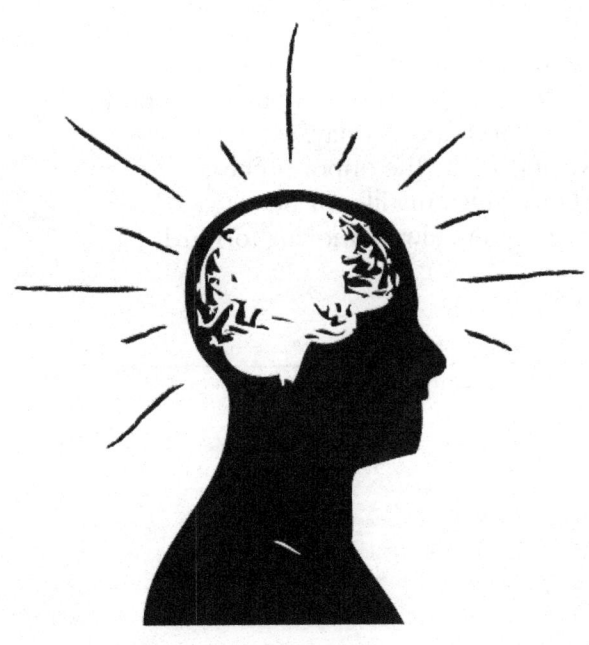

*Your strength is not in your body;
your strength is in your mind.*

Your strength is in your belief system—the belief you have in yourself and in your ability to achievement. The strength is in commitment. The strength is in your ability to say no to things that are harmful to your body, and the ability to say yes to things that are good for you. This strength is something you are born with. It increases through your challenging life. Strength is the power that rests in you, in every cell of your body, in every part of your soul, and in the depths of your mind.

Acknowledging that inner strength is all you need to success.

What power is stronger than your will? What power is stronger than the passion for life? What power is stronger then you? There is no power stronger than life force, which breathes through you every moment of your existence.

You were given the greatest strength to create the life you want to live. You were also given the greatest strength to create the body you want to have.

But you were also given free will to use your power the way you want to use it. You were given free will to use the power, or not to use the power. You were given free will to use the power in harmful ways. I know, it is ironic, isn't it, to think about the power this way. But every time you reach out for unhealthy foods, alcohol, cigarettes, drugs, you are using your strength to harm your body.

It takes the same amount of energy to say *no* and the same amount of energy to say *yes* to good or to bad things in your life—to things that will harm you or things that will benefit you.

Combining your strength and free will and redirecting them towards a balanced and healthy lifestyle is something that is completely in your power.

There are many things in life that are out of our control. Fitness is not one of them. Maintaining a healthy lifestyle and keeping a fit body are things that we CAN do. We hold the power and the strength to accomplish the ultimate. We don't even need to acquire them; we already have them. There is no need to plan, research, learn, or wait. Your power is right here, right now, waiting to act on your command, to reach whatever we desire.

Our job is merely to direct the power that we hold. Acceptance and direction of the power will create miracles in our life, will transform our body, and will empower other areas of our life with its magical wave of energies.

As our energies get redirected, the energy of waves will continue to bring health and happiness our way. The positive waves of energy will only bring good. This is why it is important to direct our energies to what is good and what brings good into our life. This is why taking care of our body is important. A good, healthy body continues to create the waves of magic, health, and wealth.

Keeping fit is not just about looking good or being healthy. Keeping fit is about respecting your life, your body, and the Creator of life, who has given you his own creating power to use. So, use it wisely!

A few rules:

You can never, ever use the words "I can't" or "It's too much, I can't do it." These have to be taken out of your vocabulary altogether. Negative remarks cannot be made—no exception under any circumstances.

You can take parts that you like out of this section and repeat them frequently when working out. You can use them during your training, especially when it gets tough. Keeping a positive mind-set and repeating positive affirmations will empower you and increase your strength instantly. Use the power of your mind to increase the strength of your body. It really does work!

Fitness Motivation:

As the tree stands strong, balanced by its roots, reaching to the sky with its strong and massive body, so am I standing balanced and empowered by the strength and power that are stronger than the power of the oldest forest tree.

As the rivers, empowered by the melting icebergs, make their way, creating new landscapes with their force, so I feel the same power of the rivers flowing through my veins.

The flowing power creating the energy so strong that nothing, nothing, stands in my way, as nothing stands in the way of a wild river, rushing, storming, destroying, and creating. So I am destroying laziness and fat, and building muscles strong and firm, the same way new landscapes are created by the wild rivers of the world.

As the ocean is empowered by its massive lengths and depths, I lay within the deepest the oceans, feeling the presence of its power. I feel no fear as the ocean builds all its power, I feel no fear as I am part and one with the power of the ocean. I let it flow, I let it be, and I let myself be part of a power that is stronger than the power of any other human being.

I feel the strength of enormous power building up in me. I feel connected with the greatest powers of the universe, the greatest powers of life, the greatest powers that always win. I am a winner; I am a winner of my own destiny.

My mind is calm and clear. I am the most powerful person in this room. I am stronger than an army of men. I am stronger than the ocean. I can create landscapes; I can destroy mountains. The power is in me, and this is power greater than life. This is power greater than me. I let the power work through my thoughts, enter my body, and manifest itself through me.

---

*I can run endlessly.
I am not controlled by the abilities of my body.
I am controlled by the abilities of my beliefs
and the strength of my mind.*

No physical challenge is too big for me. I am an extraordinary human being with extraordinary powers.

I direct my powers to create the fit body, the body that I love.

I am fit and I am strong.

I am getting stronger every day.

I am fit, healthy and I am in control of my powers.

I am in control of my life.

I take charge, I take actions, and I see results.

I welcome the most challenging regimen because I am the best in everything I do.

I am so strong I can move the tallest mountain.

15

Dreams

☆

Have the dreams so high,

That you can't reach them,

Until you become a person who can.

-Ghandi

I close my eyes as I lay in a bed of thick grass, surrounded by a deep green forest.

Tall, strong trees are stopping the light from shining through the wild branches. The small rays of light reach my face as the wind gently moves the trees. Short glimpses of sun touch my face as wind brushes through the tops of the forest trees. Fresh breeze, like a fresh breath, lights up the air and changes the presence of darkness and coldness.

I look up towards the sun, looking for a warm touch, waiting for its smile to touch my face and awaken the dream. The trees and breeze allow me to look up, straight into the gentle rays of sun, soaking up their energies. Through the protection of the branches, I tolerate the light and I can open my eyes widely and see my dreams—and I see my dreams come true. I see them clearly, shining in my life.

I reach out with my arms, playfully grasping the shining treasures of the light. Like diamonds, light is sinking through my fingers, allowing me to feel my dreams.

The dreams of my life, high above in the sky, protected by my forest of trees, are leading me, making a route for me to rise above and reach the dreams. The sun, with its warm smile gently shining down through the branches, is lighting up the way to my dreams.

I am protected by the forest,

I am led by the strokes of sunlight,

I am guided by the kind wind,

and I am encouraged by my own heart.

When the heart lights up like the sun above, the soft wind gives life to all my dreams.

Life begins in all my dreams above. The dreams awake, they begin to move, they start breathing, they are born and they become alive. They begin their journey of life. They start making the journey that I have planned, waiting for me to join them.

Dreams are always there, withing our heart, waiting for us to light them with energy of life. Dreams are waiting to be given our time and attention, so that they can manifest in our life.

Dreams are born and they live, waiting to mark their presence in our life.

Welcome your dreams, allow them to come to life, give them wings to fly, and give them love to flourish. Let the protection of your roots and life around you protect you and guide you so that you can climb, one branch at a time, towards your dream, which is already manifesting and already creating. Its in your existence.

Don't abandon your dreams to live your life on your own; they are your dreams, they are created by you, and they are meant for you.

Make your way towards that place, at the highest point of that forest tree, where the sky unlocks its doors, and you enter the world of your dreams. You live the life that has already been created by you and for you.

Dreams hold the keys to your thoughts, your energies, your heart, your love, your happiness and your life.

———————— ✦ ————————

**The dreams are here,
the doors are opened,
enter.**

———————— ✦ ————————

16

Giving

The power of giving is not just underestimated; it is simply ignored for reasons unknown to me. I am an understanding person, some would argue too understanding. But if there is one thing that I don't understand, it is that we ignore the blessings of giving, ignore hearing the cry for help, ignore denying the basics of human life to a fellow human.

It is so easy to give, so easy to part with something you call your own, but so many people find it so, so difficult, even impossible, hence they ignore it. It takes very little effort to give, yet we would rather look the other way.

All it takes is to reach into the depths of your own heart and search for kindness, compassion, and the truth.

All it takes is to reach into the depths of your soul and search for the pure love that all things are made of, including you.

Once you look, once you find that pure love, then it doesn't feel like you are giving things away. It just feels like you are sharing and benefiting yourself.

You have access to gold, but it is not yours. You have a means of discovery, but the findings are not yours alone. You have a place of birth, but you don't own it. What you have is abilities to achieve, but success is not yours alone.

You were given a heart
a heart to share,
a heart to help,
and a heart to love.

---

*A cry for life
is not a cry.*

*It is a wish
for a better life.*

*A cry for food
is not a cry.*

*It is a wish
to survive.*

*A cry for love
is a cry for love.*

*A cry for love
is a calling.*

Answer.

Give, with love.

Meditation and reflection on giving:

Every morning, the sun will rise. Every morning, the sun will give its power of heat, its power of light. There is no dispute; the sun will give, regardless.

Every night, the stars will brighten up the skies, and every night, the moon will comfort us in the darkness of the night. The stars don't ask, and the moon doesn't speak; they give, regardless.

The flowers grow and blossom, welcoming the bees. The flowers give, regardless. The bees work and give, regardless.

The trees grow in all parts of our world. Some grow under harsh conditions, yet they grow, producing fruits for us to share, regardless.

Nature does not sell; nature gives, regardless.

What makes us humans separate from this cycle of the natural world? What makes us belong and own, control and dictate? It is our own ignorance.

Rise above and awaken your awareness of the cycle of life. Share your life, share your knowledge, share your experience, and share your love.

Allow the oneness to extend and glow. This is the beginning of your freedom, the beginning of the giving; the giving and sharing, supporting and loving.

How many times have you given without asking for anything in return?

How many times have you given easily?

How many times have you given with love and a smile on your face?

How many times have you offered help, and your help was rejected?

How many times have you helped, and the help was welcomed?

How many times have you brought a smile to the face of another human being?

How many times have you brought the tears to the eyes of another human being?

To give is to give freely. To give is to give with ease. To give is to give with love, and to give with love is to give, regardless.

Just as life was given to us, regardless, so we treasure it.

Just as life was given to us, regardless, so we remember it, always.

What do we own?
What do we share?
Where are the borders?
Where is the pay?
Where is the judge to tell us all the rights and wrongs of our world today?

Simplicity of life begins with you, simplicity of love grows from you, and simplicity of giving extends from you.

Give, share, hold on to...do what you please, as long as you follow the wish of your heart.

I found blessings in volunteering work, it helped me understand things I was struggling to understand. It helped me to put my life into perspective, it opened up new opportunities, it give me all that much needed life purpose. Giving your time, your knowledge and your experiences to benefit others, will not only benefit others, but will benefit you in so many beautiful ways you could never imagine. You will receive so much more in a way of gratitude and blessings, in all different parts of your life.

Volunteering an helping others will change your life for ever.

17
Success

Meditation on success:

I recognise, that there are things in life I cannot control.

But I also recognise and accept, that success is not one of them.

Success is one thing in my life, that I know, it's in my full control and fully achievable.

I am in charge of the success in my life. I decide how successful I want to be, how successful I will be.

I decide everything about my success; when I will succeed and how successful I will be.

My desired success is resting in the centre of my heart. I feel the wining power of my success, growing and expending with every single heartbeat. I feel the vibration of the triumphal energies, flowing, creating the opportunities for success, empowering me with every bit of my heart.

I am the power of success; I am that success. I am all that I want to be. I am that magical vibration of wining power of success, I feel it in my heart, I feel in with my body and I see it with my own eyes.

And now I also believe it.

I see the success materialising right here, in front of my eyes. I see it clearly, so clearly, that I could touch it and feel it with my own hands. *(visualise your success, what does success mean to you, see it, feel it)*

No one, no one can take this away from me. No one has the power, greater than mine. I am the only person in charge of my triumphal energy, wining power and my success.

I am taking charge of the power, granted in me, and I am channelling it, making my dreams and goals the reality of my daily life. I am channelling the power of success, I am empowering the success, just the way I imagine it, just the way I feel it in my heart.

My success is within and around me. My success stays with me wherever I go.

Success just is. Here, now, always. Success is not something I chase. Success exists, just as I do, success is me, here and now.

Lets visualise your success now.

I breathe the energies of winning. Whatever I touch, whatever I attend to, I, make it a success. Today I acknowledge the success within me, today I accept the success is me, today I know my life is a success.

18

Life Purpose

Why torture ourselves with the question of our life's purpose or what the meaning of life is?

The Internet knows it all; the World Wide Web has the answers to everything.

The free encyclopaedia states that the meaning of life constitutes a philosophical question concerning life's purpose and the significance of life or our existence in general.

This concept can be expressed through a variety of related questions, such as:

Why are we here?
    What is life all about?
        What is the meaning of it all?
            What is the point?

These questions have been the subject of much philosophical, scientific, and theological speculation throughout our history. There have been a large number of answers to these questions from many different cultural and ideological backgrounds.

The meaning of life is deeply mixed with the philosophical and religious conceptions of existence, consciousness, and happiness, and it touches on many other issues, such as ontology, values, purpose, ethics, good and evil, free will, conception of God, the existence of God, and the soul.

An alternative, humancentric, and not a cosmic/religious approach is the question, "What is the meaning of my life?"
T
he value of the question pertaining to the purpose of life may coincide with the achievement of ultimate reality, or a feeling of oneness, or a feeling of sacredness.

But what does "life purpose" mean to you?

What is your life purpose? What is your meaning of life?

Meditation on the purpose of life:

When life extends its wings, and takes its different dimension, when life starts mirroring your inner self, outside your closest world, the journey of your life purpose, will begin.

When your world, stops living just for you, when your world, opens up the door and free the energy of your soul, the journey of your life purpose will begin.

One thought, that redirects from your own need, to the need of others, and your life purpose, has begun.

This wish, that was for you, is now the wish, for someone else. The caring hand, that helped you, is now helping someone else. The swift from me to you is the swift from life to purpose.

The compassion that stretches beyond your dreams, reaching and creating, is taking the form of your purpose, now.
Life purpose, the bond between you and God's divine power, the link that holds you alive.

The link that keeps the balance, the eternity, the energy of pure gratification.

And all you need to do is to extend your thought and revolve its power from your own needs to the need of another.

Create the energy, the thought, that will awaken the compassion, love and caring deeds, so purpose in your life will begin to shine, will begin to serve and will begin to live, with you and in life of those, who need it.

Select one wish, that you have wished for you,
and give it away, to someone else, today.

When life extends its wings, and takes its different dimension, when life starts mirroring your inner self, outside your closest world, the journey of your life purpose, will begin.

When your world stops living just for you, when your world, opens up the door and free the energy of soul, the journey of your life purpose will begin.

Begin your life, extend your purpose, live and live well, now.

About the Author

Every human being in this world shares the same feelings. Every human being in this world faces the same personal issues. But not every human being believes in his abilities to succeed. Not everyone believes in great potential that we all hold the key to.

www.bestcoach.tv

Petra Oblak is a Life Coach and offers her Life Coaching Services via her company www.BestCoach.tv. "Learn to Coach Yourself" is one of her most successful group coaching sessions available online and in different locations in Central London.

Petra's main quality as a life coach is her personal experience and her honesty about her life's challenges. Thought she is an extremely successful businesswoman in her own right, she has kept her humanity and spirituality through her successful career.

Following her studies at ALBO AMI University in Milan, Italy, where Petra's healing powers were measured to be the highest level quantifiable, she started her career in London as a Bioenergy Healer. However, her career took a turn when she co-funded her first broadcasting company, which dominated her working life for most of her adult life.

In her early years, Petra spent generous amount of her time surfing in Hawaii, hence the Aloha Spirit reflection in her books and coaching programs.

However, it was volunteering both in London and in Africa that contributed to the biggest and most profound changes in Petra's life. This too reflect through her coaching and her coaching workshops, demonstrating she lives her talk!

Her "Life Coaching Manual" is great addition to any Life Changing journey and is available to purchase on Amazon and on www.bestcoach.tv. You can contact Petra via the same website should you need any further support on your coaching journey.

Made in the USA
Monee, IL
12 January 2024